ONE-PARTY PRESS?

Coverage of the 1952 Presidential Campaign in 35 Daily Newspapers

By NATHAN B. BLUMBERG

UNIVERSITY OF NEBRASKA PRESS
LINCOLN, NEBRASKA

8321

Dedicated
to those members of the working press who,
a credit to their profession,
need not fear the discovery
of a brass check in their pockets.

FOREWORD

There is every reason to believe that this book will evoke vigorous comment, both pro and con. It deals with a subject—the 1952 presidential campaign and its treatment in certain newspapers—which is still an emotional storm center. This study, I believe, is thoroughly accurate and honest. It is a sound investigation, in large part allowing the data to tell their own story.

The author is a teacher and working newspaperman. Dr. Blumberg, Assistant Professor of Journalism at the University of Nebraska, served for three years as associate editor of the Lincoln *Star* and during the 1952 campaign closely watched the very campaign news that he has studied in this project. He has applied standards of judgment which are rooted in the practical problems of editing, heading up and laying out the news for the daily editions of metropolitan newspapers. To his practical experience he added the impartial techniques of orthodox academic research.

WILLIAM F. SWINDLER
Director, School of Journalism
University of Nebraska

1

THE PROBLEM

CHARGES THAT AMERICAN NEWSPAPERS ARE GUILTY OF
bias in their news columns are nothing new. Many books
and scores of articles have been written on the subject,
some in anger, some in sorrow, others in ignorance, still
others in the dispassionate spirit of scholarly objectivity.
The charge has been at one time or another, it is safe to
say, a topic of conversation for almost every adult American. Who has not heard the bromide "You can't believe
what you read in the papers"?

On the other hand, the defense of the press has been
undertaken with much the same consistency and vigor. The
major part of this defense has been made by publishers and
editors in speeches, articles and through their organs of

publicity and information. Occasionally someone who is
not and never has been a member of the working press will
rally to the cause, but these occasions have been notably,
perhaps embarrassingly, few in number.

Through the years, as any historian of journalism knows,
the American press has been regarded with varying degrees
of suspicion, distrust and, in some cases, contempt. From
the time of Benjamin Harris' *Publick Occurrences* in 1690
to the present time there have been critics, professional and
amateur, who have not hesitated to belabor newspapers for
what they regarded as serious deficiencies, and no doubt
criticisms will continue to be made so long as the press
remains free.

Some of this criticism has been merited, some has not.
Some critics have been honest, some have not. Some newspapers have benefited from the honest criticism, some have
not. And some editors and publishers are interested in the
complex problem of a newspaper's responsibilities in a free
society, some are not.

A clear fact is that criticism of newspaper conduct greatly
increases every four years as the American people partici-
pate in their quadrennial selection of a president. Occasionally there have been complaints concerning press
behavior during off-year congressional elections, but the
most important expressions of dismay have been made during and following presidential campaigns. The cry of bias
in the press has risen steadily since 1932, when Franklin D.
Roosevelt was elected and later re-elected three times despite the overwhelming editorial alignment of newspapers
against him. Charges of press bias reached a crescendo
following the unexpected victory of President Truman in

1948 with only a handful of newspapers supporting him.[1]

The defense of the press during this period of 1932 to 1948 was constructed primarily on the contention that although a majority of newspapers certainly expressed editorial preference for the Republican candidate in each election, the news columns fairly reported the activities of the Democratic candidate. Although no significant study was made of press coverage of these campaigns, careful students of newspapers generally rallied to the cause of the press on this issue.[2] It was a sad commentary on the ability of newspapers to sway public opinion on their editorial pages, but no finer defense of the press in a democratic society could be made than that news columns were not perverted to serve the ends of editorial preferences.

During the 1952 presidential election, however, the charge of press bias increased in both volume and vigor to a point never before attained. It actually became one of the issues in the campaign, being pursued with far greater em-

---

[1] Despite what some critics of the press have said, this situation was not extraordinary. In the thirty-seven presidential campaigns preceding the 1952 election, the winner had the editorial support of a majority of newspapers eighteen times and did not have it nineteen times. See Frank Luther Mott, "Has the Press Lost Its Punch?" *The Rotarian*, October, 1952, p. 13. He concludes that "there seems to be no correlation, positive or negative, between support by a majority of newspapers during a campaign and victory in a presidential canvass."

[2] The late Ralph L. Crosman, director of the University of Colorado College of Journalism and a courageous and competent critic of press behavior, nevertheless maintained that the news columns, with few exceptions, had remained free of editorial influence during the four campaigns in which Roosevelt was a presidential candidate.

phasis than in the days when FDR took to the radio for his
"fireside chats" or when President Truman excoriated newspapers from the rear platform of a railroad train as he conducted his 1948 whistle-stop tour. Although the most
bitter complaints in 1952 were made by supporters of
candidate Stevenson, several correspondents for pro-Eisenhower newspapers joined in the view that the Democratic
candidate was being given considerably less than his fair
share of coverage in newspapers throughout the country.
The expression "one-party press" found quick currency
and became an epithet to be hurled against editors and
publishers.

The cry of "one-party press" has been a source of much
confusion, misunderstanding and misinterpretation. There
actually are two aspects to the charge and they cannot be
thrown together if a rational approach to the problem is to
be made. One side of the "one-party press" coin was concerned with the predominant editorial preference of American daily newspapers for one political party. The other side
of the coin projected the view that American newspapers
allowed their editorial preferences to color, slant and dis-
tort the news columns.

These two views were expressed in concise terms by
President Truman and candidate Stevenson during the
1952 presidential campaign. An examination of their words
brings into focus the two distinct and separate charges. Mr.
Truman, in a formal statement at a press conference two
months before the election, said:

Newspapers—especially daily newspapers—have become
big business, and big business traditionally has always been

Republican. I suggest that Americans bear this in mind, and add a dash of salt to every Republican helping of news, especially in those many papers and magazines which do not give a fair balance of news between the two major parties.[3]

In other words, it is Mr. Truman's belief that most daily newspapers are pro-Republican editorially and that they are not fair to the Democrats in the news columns.

But Adlai Stevenson spoke to editors and publishers three days earlier at Portland, Ore., in these words:

> I have no doubt whatever that the bulk of owners and publishers and editors are doing an honest job with the news. I ought to know, because I am straining the impartiality of the press to the limit these days. Yet as a candidate in a hard-fought campaign, I have been impressed by the fair treatment accorded me by most newspapers, including most of those aligned editorially with the opposition. I am convinced that nearly all publishers are doing their honest best, according to their lights—even if I must confess that sometimes their lights seem to be a little dim.
>
> I am glad to pay this tribute to the press. It is true, and I think it should be said. I am grateful for the impartiality and fullness of your news columns. . . .
>
> I am in favor of a two-party system in politics. And I think we have a pretty healthy two-party system at the moment. But I am in favor of a two-party system in our press, too. And I am, frankly, considerably concerned when I see the extent to which we are developing a one-party press in a two-party country.[4]

To Mr. Stevenson, it is clear, the charge of "one-party press" applied solely to the editorial preferences of daily

[3] New York *Times*, Sept. 12, 1952, p. 13.
[4] New York *Times*, Sept. 9, 1952, p. 18.

newspapers. He paid ungrudging tribute to the news columns in "most newspapers."

Thus Mr. Truman and Mr. Stevenson agreed that the
editorial policies of daily newspapers were overwhelmingly
in favor of the Republicans. But they parted company on
the second part of the charge. The President contended
that news columns were biased while the Democratic presidential candidate maintained that in the majority of cases
he had found gratifying impartiality in news reports of the
1952 campaign.

The fact that most newspapers editorially have favored
the Republican party is beyond dispute. In this sense, as
Stevenson pointed out, we have a "one-party press." Percentages of newspapers expressing editorial preference in
the last six presidential campaigns are as follows: [5]

	Rep.	Dem.
1932	55.5%	38.7%
1936	60.4	34.5
1940	66.3	20.1
1944	60.1	22.0
1948	65.2	19.4
1952	67.3	14.5

Even more revealing is the state-by-state breakdown of
newspaper editorial support for Eisenhower in the 1952
campaign: [6]

---

[5] *Editor & Publisher*, Aug. 2, 1952, p. 48. In 1948, Thurmond
was supported by 3.8% of the newspapers and Wallace by 0.2%
so that Truman actually was supported by only 15.4%.

[6] *Editor & Publisher*, Nov. 1, 1952. This poll was completed
Oct. 27, 1952, and included 1,385 of 1,773 daily newspapers published in the United States. Total daily circulation of newspapers
in the poll was 50,013,420, or 92.59% of the total daily U.S. circulation.

State	EISENHOWER No.	EISENHOWER Circ.	STEVENSON No.	STEVENSON Circ.	INDEPENDENT OR UNDECIDED No.	INDEPENDENT OR UNDECIDED Circ.
Alabama	8	383,134	7	80,277	2	94,582
Alaska	4	12,002	..	.....	..	.....
Arizona	6	160,870	4	14,291	..	.....
Arkansas	10	74,651	9	196,655	6	48,052
California	78	3,191,339	13	558,979	8	41,270
Colorado	12	450,910	4	20,209	3	27,162
Connecticut	20	664,666	..	.....	3	24,649
Delaware	2	84,356	..	.....	..	.....
Dist. of Columbia	3	600,620	..	.....	1	226,573
Florida	13	421,868	5	167,030	6	185,084
Georgia	8	207,498	12	534,831	5	33,884
Hawaiian Islands	2	125,687	..	.....	1	10,808
Idaho	7	90,800	2	17,338	1	5,665
Illinois	52	3,488,969	4	35,420	15	121,541
Indiana	38	1,064,526	13	150,533	12	145,005
Iowa	32	758,777	2	20,084	4	37,724
Kansas	41	441,619	2	3,444	2	8,400
Kentucky	6	90,344	11	464,327	7	50,417
Louisiana	9	192,498	1	99,260	8	359,778
Maine	6	178,496	..	.....	3	55,201
Maryland	7	638,246	2	38,700	3	20,536
Massachusetts	22	1,494,921	2	115,325	11	577,563
Michigan	35	2,005,534	1	3,381	5	131,591
Minnesota	21	902,508	1	7,670	2	9,152
Mississippi	7	39,851	4	94,974	3	36,618
Missouri	26	1,269,176	13	441,708	5	16,562
Montana	8	33,736	1	29,788	2	29,217
Nebraska	15	404,873	2	30,460	2	13,664
Nevada	5	22,159	1	10,914	..	.....
New Hampshire	3	31,432	..	.....	3	52,246
New Jersey	13	765,400	1	44,038	5	181,026
New Mexico	10	68,860	1	11,985	3	14,235
New York	71	7,542,539	7	418,387	9	458,510
North Carolina	6	249,813	13	297,070	16	236,755

State	EISENHOWER No.	EISENHOWER Circ.	STEVENSON No.	STEVENSON Circ.	INDEPENDENT OR UNDECIDED No.	INDEPENDENT OR UNDECIDED Circ.
North Dakota	10	136,765	..	.....	1	5,456
Ohio	49	2,553,119	5	175,097	16	154,259
Oklahoma	18	497,665	11	70,224	14	61,778
Oregon	13	342,190	2	204,449	1	7,373
Pennsylvania	83	3,316,391	5	99,637	14	195,385
Rhode Island	4	222,221	..	.....	1	7,309
South Carolina	7	275,956	5	88,280	3	22,889
South Dakota	10	121,410	..	.....	1	16,162
Tennessee	15	700,662	3	126,893	5	33,573
Texas	38	1,563,190	13	139,650	16	356,663
Utah	1	92,365	..	.....	2	130,158
Vermont	8	78,438	..	.....	1	3,529
Virginia	16	534,378	5	62,794	9	117,902
Washington	19	823,866	1	18,749	2	15,838
West Virginia	16	279,216	8	167,124	1	11,421
Wisconsin	17	413,253	4	398,483	5	34,323
Wyoming	3	25,474	2	8,323	3	8,257
TOTALS	933	40,129,237	202	5,466,781	250	4,417,402
% OF TOTAL	67.34	80.24	14.52	10.88	18.14	8.88

It is clear, therefore, that Stevenson enjoyed an advantage in newspaper support in only three states—Georgia, Kentucky and North Carolina—and that he had no daily newspaper support in nine states—Connecticut, Delaware, Maine, New Hampshire, North Dakota, Rhode Island, South Dakota, Utah and Vermont—in addition to Alaska, Hawaii and the District of Columbia. Furthermore, he had negligible editorial support in key electoral states—New York, California, Pennsylvania, Ohio, Illinois, Massachusetts, Michigan, Indiana.

These statistics are based on the number of newspapers supporting nominees of each party. Percentages based on circulation increase the advantage of the Republicans. In 1948, for instance, while Dewey had the numerical support of 65.2% of the dailies it represented 78.5% of the circulation, while Truman had the backing of only 10% of the newspapers by circulation. Similarly, in 1952, Eisenhower had 80.24% of the support by circulation compared to 10.88% for Stevenson.

But even this statistical breakdown, nothing new to those persons who are interested in the problem, fails to provide any light on the second and more important aspect of the "one-party press" charge. Did a large number of newspapers utilize their news columns to aid the cause of the Republican candidate they supported? The argument was batted back and forth during the campaign—and it should be noted that the complaint was voiced frequently long before the election returns were in—but with virtually no practical results. Bits and pieces of evidence were offered on both sides, but they were little more than hastily conducted surveys, in many instances made not by journalists but by politicians and other partisans intimately concerned with the outcome of the election or by persons not competent to undertake an analysis of press performance. Much of the criticism was based on an obvious ignorance of the manner in which a newspaper functions, a lack of understanding of how news stories are written and edited, and the limitations of time, space and manpower that influence coverage in a daily newspaper.

Perhaps the most interesting of these campaign surveys was made by four American authors who supported Steven-

son and whose findings, published in newspapers on
October 24, created a brief flurry as election day ap-
proached. The statement on the findings was signed by 96
authors, although only four—John Hersey, John Steinbeck,
Herman Wouk and Cleveland Amory—had participated in
the hurried analysis. They reported that they had sampled
26 newspapers for a period of one week in six politically
"doubtful" states—Ohio, Massachusetts, Michigan, Illinois,
Pennsylvania and California—and that only four of the
papers had been fair in their coverage.[7] The response from

---

[7] The four newspapers in which the authors reported they found
no bias were the Boston (Mass.) Globe, Toledo (O.) Blade, Akron
(O.) Beacon-Journal and Cleveland (O.) Plain Dealer. The news-
papers allegedly guilty of distortion in the news columns were the
Chicago (Ill.) Tribune, Chicago (Ill.) Sun-Times, Chicago (Ill.)
Herald-American, Boston (Mass.) Post, Boston (Mass.) Herald,
Boston (Mass.) Daily Record and Advertiser, Dayton (O.) Daily
News, Columbus (O.) Citizen, Columbus (O.) Evening Dispatch,
Philadelphia (Pa.) Inquirer, Philadelphia (Pa.) Evening Bulletin,
Pittsburgh (Pa.) Sun-Telegraph, Pittsburgh (Pa.) Press, San Fran-
cisco (Calif.) Chronicle, San Francisco (Calif.) Examiner, Los An-
geles (Calif.) Examiner, Oakland (Calif.) Tribune, Los Angeles
(Calif.) Times, Detroit (Mich.) News, Detroit (Mich.) Free Press,
Detroit (Mich.) Times. See Editor & Publisher, Oct. 25, 1952,
p. 7, which lists only 25 newspapers. News accounts in papers of
Oct. 24 said the study was made in seven states and included the
Milwaukee (Wis.) Journal and Wisconsin State Journal of Madison. The Columbus Evening Dispatch was not mentioned in news
accounts. One of the authors told Editor & Publisher that the
Wisconsin papers had been dropped from the survey. The authors
made seven charges against the newspapers accused of distortion:
slanted writing of news stories, prejudiced use of photographs, unfavorable placement of stories concerning Democrats, inadequate
volume of coverage of Democratic news, inadequate general coverage of Democratic news, omission of stories favoring Democrats
and use of headlines reflecting meaning of stories inaccurately.

representatives of the newspapers which were not given a clean bill of health ranged from silence and patient disagreement to angry denunciations of the authors and their hasty conclusions.[8]

Lee Hills, executive editor of the Detroit *Free Press*, probably came close to summing up the approach of many amateur critics of the press, including the ninety-six authors:

> The most partisan Stevenson followers hunted proof of their suspicion because we liked Ike on our editorial (opinion) page. So they ignored the vast coverage given their man in our news columns. We could have satisfied them only by slanting the news for the Democrats.
>
> The most ardent Eisenhower supporters, on the other hand, weren't satisfied with editorial support. They complained because we didn't crusade for Ike by slanting our news columns for him.
>
> The truth seems to be that people, when strongly aroused, don't read objectively. They see what they want to see.[9]

Four of the newspapers—the Chicago *Tribune*, Philadelphia *Evening Bulletin*, Los Angeles *Times* and Detroit *News*—are included in this study of thirty-five newspapers.

[8] One comment by an editor deserves to be preserved as a masterpiece of gobbledegook. George E. Minot, managing editor of the Boston *Herald*, said: "We have consistently tried and we feel sure we have succeeded in giving equal space to both candidates, although any artificial mathematical balance of space by inches is a ridiculous measure." See St. Louis *Post-Dispatch*, Oct. 24, 1952, p. 4A. Mr. Minot apparently has devised some method of achieving "equal space" without granting equal space.

[9] Lee Hills, "The Role of a Newspaper in Political Campaigns," pamphlet reprinted from Sunday Magazine of Detroit *Free Press*, Nov. 9, 1952. The inability of the layman to measure journalistic bias was evident in an Associated Press story from Sarasota, Fla.,

In an effort to achieve a professional study, Sigma Delta
Chi, professional journalistic fraternity, officially adopted
a resolution at its 1952 national convention calling for a
survey "because numerous and grave charges have been
made that the media for the dissemination of information
were biased in their news coverage of the campaign, and the
fraternity felt these charges should not go unchallenged."
The resolution also stated that since Sigma Delta Chi has
a cross section of all media among its 22,000 members, it
was the logical organization to sponsor a study, although it
had neither the funds nor the facilities to conduct such a
survey. The intent, the resolution concluded, was "to see
whether the survey is feasible and can be financed." It was
interesting to note that the undergraduate members of the
fraternity expressed considerably more enthusiasm for the
project than did the professional members at the meeting,
although a few of the latter gave valuable support to the
resolution.

Reaction to the resolution varied. It was greeted in some
quarters with the spirit that the press had nothing to fear
if it had nothing to hide. A typical statement was that made
by Barry Bingham, editor of the Louisville *Courier-Journal*,

---

published in newspapers of Oct. 24, 1952: "Verman Kimbrough,
Saratoga County school superintendent, walked into the office of
General Manager David B. Lindsay Jr. of the Sarasota *Journal*.
The newspaper, said Kimbrough, is favoring the Republicans in
the school board campaign. He had clippings to prove it. As he
left Lindsay's office, Kimbrough bumped into Philip H. Hiss, Republican school board candidate. Hiss had clippings, too. He
wanted to complain that the *Journal* was showing favoritism to
the Democrats. The two men debated with each other. They
reached no decision . . ."

who already had gone on record in favor of a study that would "determine whether Stevenson newspapers slanted their news coverage toward Stevenson and Eisenhower newspapers toward Eisenhower." And then he added: "If the press failed in that way, it would be far better for us to expose ourselves, and try to avoid it in the future." [10] Other writers took a different view. "Ever since the election," wrote one editor, "disappointed leftists and assorted breast-beaters for Stevenson have been raising quite a hue and cry over the inadequacies and bias of the American press." [11] Wrote another editor: "I suggest that the Fair Deal boys who are bleeding their little hearts out over the election turn their attention from the many dubious and synthetic surveys of campaign press coverage and devote their energy to giving the Republicans hell." [12] Roy A. Roberts, president of the Kansas City *Star*, called proposals for a survey "tommyrot." [13] Louis LaCoss, editor of the editorial page of the St. Louis *Globe-Democrat* and the most vocal opponent of a study at the Sigma Delta Chi national convention, called it "snooping" and added that he believed "it is not within the province of this fraternity, with a major segment of undergraduate membership, to advise the publishers of America how to operate their newspapers." [14] Other news-

---

[10] Associated Press Dispatch from Alton, Ill., Nov. 9, 1952.

[11] Detroit *Free Press*, Nov. 30, 1952, p. B-4.

[12] Letter by Frank G. Trippett of the Fredericksburg (Va.) *Free Lance-Star* in *Editor & Publisher*, Nov. 29, 1952, p. 4.

[13] *Editor & Publisher*, Nov. 29, 1952, p. 7.

[14] *Ibid.*, p. 34. It should be pointed out that this view of the press as a purely business enterprise with no special responsibility is shared by some editors and publishers. They regard the newspaper as a commercial product, offered for sale in much the same

papers expressed similar sentiments in their editorial columns. The gist of these writings was that anyone who wondered whether there was a basis for charges of bias against newspapers must be either a "breastbeater," a "bleeding heart," or a "New Dealer"—with or without the descriptive "leftist" or "left-wing" before the noun. It never occurred to these men—or if it did they did not allow the idea to get around—that something other than a partisan political concern might be motivating those who wanted a study of press performance during the campaign.

Nothing came of the resolution. A committee was established by Lee Hills, president of Sigma Delta Chi, to look into the possibility of a "thorough and objective" study, possibly aided by a major foundation. J. Donald Ferguson of the Milwaukee *Journal* was appointed chairman and members were Bingham, Turner Catledge of the New York *Times*, Benjamin M. McKelway of the Washington *Star*, Edward R. Murrow of the Columbia Broadcasting System, Carson F. Lyman of *U.S. News & World Report* and Dean Earl English of the University of Missouri School of Journalism. Early in 1953 the committee reported, with Bingham dissenting, that it was "not feasible" to undertake a study of press performance in the 1952 campaign. "The committee knows of no formulae," the report stated, "that would meet the magnitude and complexities of the problem of evaluating the fairness of public information media in their news coverage of the 1952 campaign." [15] The execu-

---

way that a suit of clothes is made available for purchase. As a result, they resent anyone telling them how to run their business.

[15] Supplement to *The Quill*, June, 1953, p. 1. Murrow, while unable to attend a meeting of the committee in Washington in

tive council of Sigma Delta Chi accepted the majority report of the committee and the proposed study was abandoned by the national organization of professional journalists.[16]

The American Society of Newspaper Editors and the American Newspaper Publishers Association did not even give serious consideration to a study of the press during the campaign.[17]

The course of action adopted by these three major organizations of journalism prompted Irving Dilliard, editor of the editorial page of the St. Louis *Post-Dispatch* and a former national president of Sigma Delta Chi, to a biting criticism of the press in terms of a double standard:

> The press tends to have one standard when it measures the performance of officials and public figures, and another standard when it comes to measuring its own performance. Indeed many editors and publishers do not think one newspaper has any business criticising another. Or to put it another way, the press holds other institutions up to searching

---

February, "concurred by mail with respect to the difficulty of surveying the radio and television coverage of the campaign."

[16] There was an interesting aftermath at the 1953 national convention of Sigma Delta Chi in St. Louis. A resolution urging that a study of press performance in the campaign be undertaken as soon as possible did not reach the floor of the convention. The resolutions committee substituted an innocuous resolution calling for more research into the problem of methodology. The words of Past President Irving Dilliard, who delivered the keynote address at the convention, likewise had little effect. "I happen to believe," Dilliard told the delegates, "that a survey is even more needed in 1953 than it was in 1952."

[17] For a revealing thirty-six-line account of how the A.S.N.E. handled this problem see *Problems of Journalism: Proceedings of the American Society of Newspaper Editors, 1953*, pp. 184-85.

scrutiny but is unwilling to have the same scrutiny applied to itself.[18]

Alan Barth, editorial writer for the Washington *Post*, called for a "tough and searching study" that "ought not to be cavalierly dismissed by the press." [19] Eric Sevareid, news commentator for the Columbia Broadcasting System, was caustic in his comments. Referring to "a sudden rash of news cheating such as we have not known for years" during the election campaign, Sevareid said:

> The truth must be faced: Dozens of excellent newspapers, with a record of honorable news handling, cheated in their allotment of news and picture space as between the two candidates. I do not believe the election result would have been any different, even had absolute fairness ruled, but that does not erase this blot on the record. I wish American editors had gone ahead with the self-investigation of that performance that Sigma Delta Chi and others urged; but I knew they would not, because the general finding, if sought with ruthless honesty, was a foregone conclusion and would have been too painful.[20]

These were typical comments by those who desired a study to be made. But the official publication of Sigma

---

[18] Irving Dilliard, "The Press and the Bill of Rights," *Nieman Reports*, January, 1954, p. 14. This article was from the second annual Lovejoy Lecture delivered at Colby College on Nov. 5, 1953.

[19] Alan Barth, "The Heat of the Headlines," *Nieman Reports*, April, 1953, p. 9.

[20] Eric Sevareid, "The Big Truth," pamphlet published by the School of Journalism of the University of Minnesota, and the Twin Cities Local of the American Newspaper Guild, 1953. This was the seventh annual memorial lecture delivered in Minneapolis on Oct. 23, 1953.

Delta Chi, *The Quill*, viewed differently the decision to abandon the study. It approved the reasoning of a majority of the committee and expressed regrets that the survey was not "clearly feasible" or "practicable." [21] *Editor & Publisher*, frequently called the "bible" of the newspaper profession, drew a similar conclusion. This publication had been the first to call for a study, and it felt a special interest in the matter. On November 1, 1952, *Editor & Publisher* had stated in a lead editorial:

> We think the nation's press is entitled to a fair trial—an impartial, extensive, scientific study to reveal the exact degree of fairness, or lack of it, in this presidential campaign. Too many accusations have been leveled against the press in this campaign, many for political reasons, most of them based on little if any evidence, to overlook them and forget them after Election Day. The public won't forget them—there are too many people interested in not letting them forget them.
>
> We think the American Society of Newspaper Editors should authorize a complete study and review of the kind we suggest. It will take many months and cost considerable money. But it should be done.
>
> *Editor & Publisher* is willing to contribute to the cost of an impartial analysis.[22]

Two weeks later, *Editor & Publisher* in another lead editorial, "Study Still Needed," reminded its readers that its suggestion should not be forgotten.[23] It wrote on the subject again in lead editorials the following two weeks, the latter one disagreeing with critics of the survey, including

---

[21] *The Quill*, August, 1953, p. 3.

[22] *Editor & Publisher*, Nov. 1, 1952, p. 42.

[23] *Ibid.*, Nov. 15, 1952, p. 38.

Roy A. Roberts and Louis LaCoss, and commending Sigma
Delta Chi for its resolution.[24] A few weeks later another
lead editorial hailed the appointment of the Sigma Delta
Chi committee to look into the possibility of a survey and
observed: "So far, Sigma Delta Chi is on the right track." [25]

But the enthusiasm cooled. On March 21, 1953, the
editor proclaimed in his column that "there was once great
interest in the proposed study of press fairness during the
1952 political campaign. But as the campaign fades into
limbo and the political scene gets back to normal that interest is fading obviously." [26] Then following the announcement of the Sigma Delta Chi committee that it regarded
a study as "not feasible," *Editor & Publisher* stated editorially that it still wished there could be a study, "but in
view of the inadequacy of presently-known survey methods
we must agree with the conclusion of the Sigma Delta Chi
committee that such a study is 'not feasible' at this time." [27]

This writer agreed with those who believed that unless a
comprehensive study of press performance during the 1952
campaign were undertaken, unfounded charges and coun-
ter-charges would continue to be made on all sides. The
American press, which has an admirable record of digging
out facts on many important issues, was performing no
service either to the public or to itself when it dismissed the
charges of news bias or contended that because there was
no "methodology" for measuring bias a study was not
"feasible." Certainly bias cannot be measured with a pica

[24] *Ibid.*, Nov. 22, 1952, p. 38, and Nov. 29, 1952, p. 34.
[25] *Ibid.*, Dec. 27, 1952, p. 28.
[26] *Ibid.*, March 21, 1953, p. 84. ·
[27] *Ibid.*, April 25, 1953, p. 78.

pole, and just as certainly there could be no "scientific" method of "proving" the existence of bias. Some journalists fell into the same line of thought which has plagued many academicians, attempting to create a "science" of something which is not and never will be a science.

There were some questions, this writer believed, that could be answered by a survey employing techniques that would be fair to the newspapers and yet provide a satisfactory test of their performance. In November, 1953, he began work on this study.

2

AN ANSWER

REMARKABLY FEW STUDIES OF PRESS PERFORMANCE DURING the 1952 political campaign have been made, despite the many words which have been spoken and written on the subject. Some newspapers examined and reported on their own performance. Several statewide studies have been undertaken, notably those of Florida and Wisconsin newspapers, but they were too limited in scope to lead to any valid conclusions when applied on a national scale.[1] Other attempts to analyze press performance in the 1952 cam-

---

[1] See Sidney Kobre, "How Florida Dailies Handled the 1952 Presidential Campaign," *Journalism Quarterly*, 30:163 (Spring, 1953), and Charles E. Higbie, "Wisconsin Dailies in the 1952 Campaign: Space vs. Display," *Journalism Quarterly*, 31:56 (Winter, 1954).

paign were singularly lacking in documentation and acceptable research techniques, although occasionally some
profitable information emerged from the hastily-written
articles.[2] And very little had been done to establish ways

---

[2] See especially *The Reporter*, Nov. 25, 1952. The article of most
value is Robert Lasch, "Pride and Prejudice: The Fourth Estate,"
which contains an analysis of the San Francisco *Chronicle* during
a 10-day period, applying some of the methods used in this study.
(An interesting contrast is afforded by the San Francisco *Chronicle's* self-conducted quantitative analysis, which concluded that
there was no bias in the paper's news columns. See *Editor & Publisher*, Nov. 15, 1952, p. 11.) Typical of the confusion in this magazine presentation were the diametrically opposed positions taken
by the author of an article on New York newspapers during the
campaign, and by the editor of the magazine. An editorial, "What's
Wrong With the Press?" endeavored to show that the source of
advertising revenue forces every publication to consolidate its own
monopoly on its audience, which explains "why even a paper like
the New York *Times*, which has a monopoly established by its
excellence, can grow sluggish and, in the turmoil of an election,
falter in checking the news it carries." (pp. 4-5.) But M. R. Werner,
in "New York Newspapers—6 to 1 Against Stevenson," wrote:
"The *Times* coverage of the campaign won many of its readers'
plaudits for completeness and impartiality. .... The *Times* seemed
to be bending over backward to make up for other occasions in
the past when it had not been so impartial." (p. 13.) See also Jean
Begeman, "The One-Party Press Pays Off," *The New Republic*,
Nov. 17, 1952, p. 17. This article draws sweeping conclusions on
the basis of limited and selective evidence. The survey included
twenty-one "representative newspapers" selected at random and
covered the period from Sept. 1 to Oct. 31, 1952. Five major
charges were made: Eisenhower was given top headlines, favorable
Democratic news was buried and unfavorable Democratic news
was played up, editorializing was practiced in headlines, the Republicans were favored in comparable news events, and campaign
pictures were employed to the credit of Eisenhower and the dis-
advantage of Stevenson.

and means of evaluating newspaper performance, despite some attempts at a project of this kind.[3]

A major problem was devising an acceptable sample of daily newspapers that would be large enough to produce significant data and yet be small enough to provide a workable project. The sampling employed in this study was based on an attempt to obtain a geographical distribution of newspapers most likely to have had an important influence in their respective states.[4] The original plan was to examine newspapers with the largest circulation in each of the 48 states on the assumption that this would provide a good cross-section of the American press, but for various reasons, primarily the difficulty of obtaining copies or microfilms of desired papers, it was not possible to include newspapers from 13 states. In six cases it was found necessary to substitute another large newspaper, usually with the second highest circulation in the state.

This sample resulted in a representative distribution of newspapers on the basis of editorial political preference in the 1952 election. According to the final pre-election poll by *Editor & Publisher* covering 1,385 daily newspapers,

---

[3] See especially Kenneth P. Adler, "Can Bias Be Measured?" *The Quill*, April, 1953, p. 8. This suggested method for newspaper analysis is extremely complicated and would require a large staff.

[4] It could be argued, as it has many times, that metropolitan daily newspapers are more sensational and irresponsible than newspapers in smaller towns. On the other hand, Robert H. Estabrook, editor of the editorial page of the Washington *Post*, told University of Nebraska students it was his impression that slanting of news "was found more among the smaller papers than among the larger." See Robert H. Estabrook, "Press Performance in the Campaign," *Nieman Reports*, January, 1953, p. 11.

67.34% of the papers with 80.24% of the circulation supported Eisenhower, 14.52% with 10.88% of the circulation
supported Stevenson, and 18.14% with 8.88% of the circulation declared an independent or undecided policy in
the election. In this study, 74.29% of the newspapers with
78.71% of the total daily circulation supported Eisenhower,
20% with 17.76% of the circulation supported Stevenson,
and 5.71% with 3.53% of the circulation announced an
independent or undecided editorial policy in the election.
Although the 35 newspapers comprised only 1.97% of the
total number of daily newspapers in the United States, they
had a total circulation of 7,505,070, or 13.89% of the total
circulation of United States daily newspapers.

Newspapers examined were the Birmingham (Ala.) News,
Phoenix (Ariz.) Gazette, Los Angeles (Calif.) Times,
Denver (Colo.) Post, Hartford (Conn.) Times, Wilmington (Del.) Journal-Every Evening, Miami (Fla.) Herald,
Atlanta (Ga.) Journal, Boise Idaho Daily Statesman, Chicago (Ill.) Tribune, Indianapolis (Ind.) Star, Des Moines
(Ia.) Register, Louisville (Ky.) Courier-Journal, New
Orleans (La.) Times-Picayune, Bangor (Me.) News, Baltimore (Md.) Sun, Detroit (Mich.) News, Minneapolis
(Minn.) Star, Jackson (Miss.) Clarion Ledger, St. Louis
(Mo.) Post-Dispatch, Great Falls (Mont.) Tribune, Omaha
(Neb.) World-Herald, New York (N.Y.) Times, Fargo
(N.D.) Forum, Portland (Ore.) Oregonian, Philadelphia
(Pa.) Bulletin, Sioux Falls (S.D.) Argus-Leader, Memphis
(Tenn.) Commercial Appeal, Dallas (Tex.) Morning News,
Salt Lake City, Utah Deseret News, Burlington (Vt.) Free
Press, Richmond (Va.) Times-Dispatch, Seattle (Wash.)

Post-Intelligencer, Charleston (W.Va.) *Gazette,* Milwaukee (Wis.) *Journal.*

The circulation of these newspapers ranged from 21,749 for the smallest to 925,122 for the largest, including only the morning or evening edition examined of newspapers which publish both day and night editions. Six of the newspapers have circulations under 50,000; six are between 50,-000 and 100,000; fifteen are between 100,000 and 250,000; five are between 250,000 and 500,000, and three are between 500,000 and one million.[5]

The sample, by chance, included one newspaper from each of five major chains—Hearst (Seattle *Post-Intelligencer*), Scripps-Howard (Memphis *Commercial Appeal*), Gannett (Hartford *Times*), McCormick-Patterson (Chicago *Tribune*), and Knight (Miami *Herald*)—two Pulliam newspapers (Indianapolis *Star*, Phoenix *Gazette*), and two Cowles papers (Minneapolis *Star* and Des Moines *Register*).

The final 30 days of the campaign preceding the election, October 6 to November 4, was the period selected for the survey. Front pages of the newspapers were carefully examined and a study made of inside pages on three selected dates—October 16, October 24, November 3—chosen because they are well-spaced and represent days on which there were no especially important political developments which would favor one party. When inside page coverage on one of the dates was influenced by local conditions, usually the visit to a city by one of the principals in the campaign, another issue was substituted.

[5] All circulation data in this section based on *Editor & Publisher International Year Book,* 1952.

The quantitative analysis of the newspapers was made less difficult by the fact that the use of the space unit in studies of this kind has been well established. The column-inch is a space unit common to all newspapers and affords a fair method by which to measure the amount—but not the content—of material. Unfortunately, however, the space unit has not been correctly applied in some studies which have assumed that the opinion-influencing value of an item is a function of its length. This assumption leads to the conclusion that a longer article is per se more effective than a shorter one, a conclusion which anyone who has ever served on a copy desk knows is not necessarily the case. For one thing, a journalistic law of diminishing returns has been proved in many readership studies, and it applies especially to long articles. More readers are likely to read a feature item reporting an offhand remark by a presidential candidate than will follow to the end an 18-inch story on a campaign speech. The little item, however, may well have given readers an impression of the candidate that could not be obtained from the report of his speech.

The column-inch space unit, therefore, is not a final determinant of news presentation. It provides a guide to further analysis, and correctly employed with other measurements, can be valuable in a study of newspaper performance. In this report other factors were also taken into consideration.

To arrive at the conclusions in this study, evaluation first was made of the categories of the statistical table: number of stories, column-inches of news space, number of photographs, column-inches of photograph space, number of multi-column headlines and total column-inches of space.

Then the statistical results of inside page coverage in three issues, including the same categories, were examined to see whether there were any significant differences between front page and inside page treatment. Display (primarily banner headlines or top play headlines), position of stories and examples of partiality were then appraised. Finally, consideration was given to special circumstances (for example, the visit to a newspaper's city by only one of the presidential candidates) which would justify a subjective judgment altering the statistical findings.

In the statistical analysis, stories and headlines were measured by column-inches to the nearest half-inch. Thus a three-column headline one inch deep and a 7½-inch story would be tabulated as 10½ column-inches of space. Photographs, including caption and cutline, were similarly computed. Microfilms were used in 33 of the 35 cases, and some minor differences in measurement may have resulted but they would have no effect on the individual newspaper analysis since all variations would be proportional. When more than one edition had been preserved on microfilm an effort was made to select the home delivery edition.

There were, of course, numerous problems involved in both the quantitative and qualitative sections. Some headlines and stories do not fit easily into categories established for the purpose of quantitative analysis. How, for instance, should one tabulate the headline, "Jersey Workers Boo Eisenhower"? Certainly the headline could not be listed as favorable to the Republican presidential candidate, but the story, following a lead on which the headline was based, reported in favorable terms a speech delivered by Eisenhower.

An egg is thrown at Stevenson, and the incident makes an interesting feature story. Taft narrowly escapes injury when an elevator falls. The Democratic National Committee reports that its fund drive is lagging. Nixon becomes angry at some hecklers. Democratic National Chairman Mitchell fires an assistant for allegedly helping to negotiate a government contract for a Portuguese tungsten firm. A clock falls from a temporary stand in a television studio, scratching Eisenhower's head. Republican officials gleefully report a train platform slip of the tongue by Truman, in which he is reported as thanking his listeners for coming "to look at the—the man who is running the campaign for president."

Or this one: "SAN FRANCISCO (AP)—Sen. Estes Kefauver, arriving here to speak in behalf of the Democratic presidential ticket, said Wednesday he thought President Truman's whistle-stop tour has had a 'negative effect' for Governor Adlai Stevenson."

Obviously a subjective judgment had to be made in each case. The fundamental consideration at all times was whether a story could be included in good conscience in either the Democratic or Republican column. Critics may quarrel with the decision made in some cases, but the interpretation of news reports has always been a subject of debate and it will neither surprise nor disappoint the writer if there is honest disagreement with his evaluations. In any event, the study was sufficiently extensive that the final statistical tabulation for each newspaper would not be altered appreciably if all—or none—of these stories had been included in the computations.

The qualitative appraisal presented difficulties of a different kind. Proximity is a major determinant of news, and the visit of a campaign principal of either party to any city normally would result in heavier coverage in the newspapers of that locality. There was no special problem when both presidential candidates spoke in cities where newspapers included in this study are published. On the contrary, a comparative analysis of treatment accorded visits and speeches of the two candidates often served as an excellent guide in determining whether bias was present. But complications arose when only one presidential candidate appeared in a particular locality during the period under study. Every effort was made in the qualitative analysis of individual newspaper performance to compensate for an understandable statistical imbalance which would result from a situation of this kind.

Closely related is the problem of special local interest in one of the major principals. Certainly the utterances of Nixon generally are of greater interest in California than in Florida. A newspaper in Missouri might be expected to devote more space to Truman than would a newspaper in North Dakota, and southern newspapers possibly would follow the activities of Sparkman with more than ordinary interest. The fact that Eisenhower made his campaign headquarters in Denver understandably would influence coverage of a newspaper published in that city.

Also involved were more subtle influences on newspaper coverage which defy interpretation by a ruler but which would be recognized by anyone who has served on a copy desk. The fact that a state has a tradition of preference for one of the major political parties, thereby creating a group of incumbents whose names and statements are more "newsworthy," frequently would affect coverage and display. Similarly, the words of a president of the United States normally would command more news space than the speeches of a "truth squad" dispatched to follow on the heels of the chief executive. In this campaign the problem was particularly acute, since editors were faced with the necessity of reporting President Truman's activities in addition to those of the candidates. In some instances heavier coverage of the Democrats could be explained by the numerous stories related to Truman's speeches. And occasionally specific local conditions will influence news play—properly so—a factor which a critic who lacks newspaper experience might fail to recognize.

These factors, and others similar to them, were utilized to make an evaluation of the statistical findings whenever possible. Many subjective decisions, some of them made only after months of pondering the problems, were necessary before the conclusion of this survey.

Perhaps a classic example of the difficulties presented in a study of press bias during a political campaign is contained in the so-called "Nixon fund" episode which erupted during the 1952 presidential campaign. Since the story "broke" and was resolved before the period covered in this study, it had no influence on the findings in these pages, but it stands nevertheless as an example of a thorny problem confronting anyone attempting to appraise newspaper coverage. It was a story that by its conflict, drama, human interest and possible consequence dictated prominent and extensive display. But could it be regarded as "favorable" or "unfavorable" to one side or the other? Could it not aid ᴄᴏ ᴘ y during one phase and help the other party at another time? Should it be included with the normal, traditional coverage of political campaign news—something that went into temporary eclipse while the controversy raged? These and many other questions contain elements which require further and extensive research by those persons interested in the conduct and performance of newspapers.

Special attention should be drawn to the fact that stories related to two events during the month preceding the election—the release of figures on Eisenhower's income over a ten-year period and Stevenson's emergency flight to help quell the Illinois State prison riot—were not included in this study. A pilot survey, made before this study was undertaken, revealed that most newspapers played these stories in addition to or separate from the main body of campaign news. A check of the statistical results shows that even if these two stories—each involving one of the candidates—had been included in the study it would have made only a slight difference in the final tabulations of the thirty-five newspapers.

It should also be pointed out that editorial page items, syndicated or special columns, series by the wire services or the newspapers attempting to analyze election trends, and results of professional polls were not included. Similarly, news accounts pertaining to state or local campaigns were not counted unless they clearly applied primarily to national issues involving the political fortunes of the presidential candidates.

Most important of all, perhaps, is the fact that front page items which were clearly of an editorial nature—editorials, cartoons, political cartoon strips, regularly published columns and the like—were not included in either the quantitative or qualitative analyses. It is certain, however, that a considerable part of the layman's criticism of news coverage is directed at this kind of editorial expression on what are traditionally regarded as news, not opinion, pages.

Each newspaper was ultimately placed in one of three categories:

1) *No evidence of partiality in news columns:* Newspapers which more extensively covered the activities of the candidate they editorially opposed or were above reproach for their coverage of the campaign.

2) *No conclusive evidence of partiality in news columns:* Newspapers which may appear to have given more extensive coverage to the candidate of their editorial preference, but for which there were extenuating circumstances or special cases which would not justify a charge of bias against them.

3) *Evidence of partiality in news columns:* Newspapers which clearly gave more extensive coverage to the candidate of their choice.

One final word on the methods employed in this study: They constitute an experiment, an attempt to discover whether it is possible to determine the existence of bias in news columns. The task set was not complicated by the kind of pseudo-scientific interpretations which plague too many studies of this kind. The writer leaves the unlimited ramifications of content analysis, for example, to those whose interests lie in that direction. And for all the unanswered questions—many of them posed by friends on newspapers and by faculty colleagues—the writer offers his recognition but not his apologies. This study has limitations and defects, certainly, but it should be only the first of a series of comprehensive studies of newspaper performance on a national scale. Can bias be measured? No. Can bias be scientifically "proved"? No. Is it possible to determine the existence of bias?

Yes.

3

THE FINDINGS

THE PRIMARY PURPOSE OF THIS STUDY WAS TO DETERMINE whether a significant number of newspapers demonstrated partiality in their columns in favor of the candidate they supported in the 1952 election. Secondarily there has been an attempt to appraise the performance of each newspaper in the study with the hope that, perhaps, it would point to an improvement in the performance of the American press, a goal which should be shared by schools of journalism and newspapermen alike. Two points—the expression of editorial opinion on the front page and methods of presenting campaign news—will be covered in separate articles.

All of the research involved in this study was done by the

writer, and no other person is in any way responsible for the findings.

Following are the three major general conclusions emerging from this study:

1. Of the twenty-six pro-Eisenhower newspapers examined, eleven gave the Democrats more front page space, fifteen gave the Republicans more front page space.

All seven pro-Stevenson newspapers gave the Democrats more front page space.

One of the two newspapers which announced an independent editorial policy gave the Democrats more space, the other gave the Republicans more space.

2. After both quantitative and qualitative judgments were made, fifteen pro-Eisenhower newspapers were regarded as showing no partiality, four were determined to have demonstrated partiality in favor of their candidate, and seven provided no conclusive evidence of partiality.

Among the pro-Stevenson newspapers, two showed no partiality, two showed partiality in favor of their candidate, and three gave no conclusive evidence of partiality.

Of the two newspapers which took an independent editorial position, one showed no news column partiality and one provided insufficient evidence to warrant a conclusion of partiality.

3. Six of the thirty-five newspapers examined, therefore, provided evidence of partiality in their news columns.

Specifically, it can be stated that there was slanting in the news columns during the 1952 election, but it was not as widespread as some critics have maintained. A majority of the newspapers in this study—eighteen—met the highest standards of fair news presentation, and a large number of newspapers—eleven—showed no significant degree of partiality that would warrant a change of unfairness. The six newspapers found to have demonstrated partiality in their news columns constitute a minority.

It also is evident that newspapers which supported the Republican presidential candidate performed, on the whole, at a higher level than did the pro-Democratic newspapers. If this finding is somewhat surprising, it should provide food for thought for all newspapermen. Of the thirty-three newspapers which took an editorial stand on the campaign, twenty-two gave a greater amount of front page coverage to the candidate they supported, another factor which appears significant.

NO EVIDENCE OF PARTIALITY IN NEWS COLUMNS

Newspapers supporting Eisenhower: Baltimore (Md.) *Sun,* Birmingham (Ala.) *News,* Boise *Idaho Daily Statesman,* Burlington (Vt.) *Free-Press,* Des Moines (Ia.) *Register,* Fargo (N.D.) *Forum,* Hartford (Conn.) *Times,* Memphis (Tenn.) *Commercial Appeal,* Miami (Fla.) *Herald,* Minneapolis (Minn.) *Star,* New York (N.Y.) *Times,* Philadelphia (Pa.) *Evening Bulletin,* Portland (Ore.) *Oregonian,* Richmond (Va.) *Times-Dispatch,* Wilmington (Del.) *Journal-Every Evening.*

Newspapers supporting Stevenson: Jackson (Miss.) *Clarion-Ledger,* Louisville (Ky.) *Courier-Journal.*

Independent Newspapers: Salt Lake City, Utah *Deseret News.*

NO CONCLUSIVE EVIDENCE OF PARTIALITY IN NEWS COLUMNS

Newspapers supporting Eisenhower: Bangor (Me.) *News,* Dallas (Tex.) *Morning News,* Denver (Colo.) *Post,* Detroit

(Mich.) *News,* Omaha (Neb.) *World-Herald,* Phoenix (Ariz.) *Gazette,* Seattle (Wash.) *Post-Intelligencer.*

Newspapers supporting Stevenson: Atlanta (Ga.) *Journal,* Milwaukee (Wis.) *Journal,* St. Louis (Mo.) *Post-Dispatch.*

Independent Newspapers: New Orleans (La.) *Times-Picayune.*

EVIDENCE OF PARTIALITY IN NEWS COLUMNS

Newspapers supporting Eisenhower: Chicago (Ill.) *Tribune,* Indianapolis (Ind.) *Star,* Los Angeles (Calif.) *Times,* Sioux Falls (S.D.) *Argus-Leader.*

Newspapers supporting Stevenson: Charleston (W. Va.) *Gazette,* Great Falls (Mont.) *Tribune.*

The analysis of individual newspapers includes the front pages of each newspaper from October 6 through November 4, 1952, and inside pages of October 16, October 24 and November 3, unless otherwise indicated.

Newspapers are listed alphabetically by states.

ALABAMA
BIRMINGHAM NEWS
(Eisenhower)

	Front Page		Inside Pages	
	REP.	DEM.	REP.	DEM.
Number of stories	45	56	17	19
Column-inches stories	346	464½	138½	145½
Number of photographs	6	7	2	2
Column-inches photographs	56	46	8	13
Multi-column headlines	18	20	4	4
Total column-inches news space	402	510½	146½	158½

Excellent presentation of campaign news marked the performance of the Birmingham *News* during the month preceding the 1952 election. Pro-Eisenhower editorially, this newspaper was extremely fair to both sides in its news columns.

The statistical superiority of the Democrats was largely the result of the fact that Sparkman was the only major principal to speak in Birmingham during this period. This advantage was offset by news display which tended to favor the Republicans slightly. The Republicans received top play six times, the Democrats three times, but in a majority of issues the device of equal typographical play was employed.

It should be noted that the inside pages of this newspaper constitute an extraordinary case of impartial allotment of news space. Coupled with the obvious fairness of front page presentation, this performance was outstanding.

ARIZONA
PHOENIX GAZETTE
(Eisenhower)

	Front Page*		Inside Pages	
	REP.	DEM.	REP.	DEM.
Number of stories	32	21	11	10
Column-inches stories	229	136	127½	181½
Number of photographs	8	3	1	0
Column-inches photographs	147	41	19	0
Multi-column headlines	12	2	3	3
Total column-inches news space	376	177	146½	181½

* No Sunday edition.

The apparent statistical imbalance in the above table requires careful analysis in order to appraise the perform-ance of this newspaper during the month preceding the 1952 election. Eisenhower came to Phoenix early in Octo-ber and the *Gazette* did not have an opportunity during this period to give equal local publicity in its news columns for the Democratic presidential candidate. From October 6 to October 10, the day on which Eisenhower's speech was reported, the *Gazette* ran thirteen stories totaling 98½ inches, seven photographs totaling 123 inches, and seven multi-column headlines. Included was a skyline over its nameplate on October 9 reading: "Ike Will Arrive At Montgomery Stadium At 9:25 Tomorrow Morning; Let's Be There To Say 'Howdy.'" And below a three-column photograph on its front page the same day appeared the legend: "The friendly, down-to-earth personality that has endeared Dwight D. Eisenhower to all America is reflected in this portrait . . ."

Editorial partisanship in the news columns? Most cer-tainly.

But there are modifying factors to be considered before making a final judgment on this newspaper's pre-election reporting of the campaign. If one analyzes the period fol-lowing Eisenhower's visit until the day of balloting, the *Gazette* looks infinitely more fair in its presentation. Here is the statistical breakdown on front pages from October 13 through November 4:

	REP.	DEM.
Number of stories	13	15
Column-inches stories	100	97
Number of photographs	1	3

Column-inches photographs	24	41
Multi-column headlines	3	2
Total column-inches news space	124	138

Partisanship in the news columns? Hardly.

Also to the credit of this newspaper is evidence of fairness in its inside page coverage, to which the table attests. On the debit side of the ledger is the fact that stories reporting on the Republicans were consistently given better display and position.

The *Gazette* gave front page news and photographic coverage on November 1 to a "protest march" by university students who believed that the paper was unfair in its reporting of campaign news. The students perhaps recalled front page reporting on "Ike Day." The three weeks before election day, however, were marked by fair reporting of campaign news.

CALIFORNIA

LOS ANGELES TIMES

(Eisenhower)

	Front Page		Inside Pages	
	REP.	DEM.	REP.	DEM.
Number of stories	59	39	30	18
Column-inches stories	660	387½	380	309½
Number of photographs	5	2	6	4
Column-inches photographs	115	39	114	66
Multi-column headlines	26	13	16	13
Total column-inches news space	775	426½	494	375½

This newspaper gave far greater coverage to the candidate it supported in its reporting of the 1952 presidential campaign. The Republicans were given better display and overwhelmingly greater photographic and news treatment.

The statistics tell a large part of the story, but they fail to convey the day-by-day effect of reporting of this kind. The slant given to headlines, consistently better and more comprehensive play for one side, political announcements run as news stories, the matter-of-fact reporting of Democratic activities and colorful coverage of similar Republican activities—all of these add up to a distinct appearance of favoritism in the news columns.

Contrast, for instance, coverage given to the visits of the two major candidates to Los Angeles one week apart.

Day Preceding Arrival in Los Angeles

Stevenson: one-column headline in fifth column below the fold, 4½-inch story.

Eisenhower: one-column headline at top of third column, 13-inch story.

Day of Arrival

Stevenson: one-column headline at top of fourth column, 10½-inch story; insert informing readers a map of the motorcade route can be found elsewhere in the paper; one-column head in fifth column at the fold on Stevenson's San Francisco speech, 6-inch story; one-inch story announcing that Stevenson would speak on the radio in Los Angeles that evening. (These stories were played against a three-column photograph of Eisenhower and a two-column all-capital headline with two-column deck and two-column lead on 9½-inch story, reporting an Eisenhower speech in the South.)

Eisenhower: four-column top headline with one-column deck and 11½-inch story; two-column map of the motorcade route; two-column head above fold on Eisenhower's San Francisco speech, 8-inch story; two-column headline on schedule of the day's activities, 7-inch story; three-column photograph of Eisenhower in San Francisco. (These were played against a one-column headline at top of fourth column on a Stevenson speech, 13½-inch story.)

Day Following Speech

Stevenson: five-column top headline, two-column deck, 12½-inch story; three-column headline, 9-inch story; one-column headline, 6-inch story; one-column headline, 1-inch story; three-column photograph, 8 inches deep.

Eisenhower: eight-column banner, six-column deck, one-column second deck, 12½-inch story; another one-column second deck, 14-inch story; three-column headline, 11-inch story; two-column headline, 4-inch story; one-column headline, 5½-inch story; four-column photograph, 10 inches deep.

Incidentally, a classic illustration of the utilization of the society section for political purposes is contained in this newspaper during the period under consideration. These numerous stories were not included in the statistical computation, of course, but they probably would astonish anyone who had never seen this section of the Los Angeles Times.

COLORADO
DENVER POST
(Eisenhower)

	Front Page		Inside Pages	
	REP.	DEM.	REP.	DEM.
Number of stories	35	32	29	21
Column-inches stories	408	316	320	222½
Number of photographs	1	0	5	3
Column-inches photographs	18	0	67	32
Multi-column headlines	22	11	14	10
Total column-inches news space	426	316	387	254½

There are circumstances modifying the fact that the Republicans enjoyed an advantage in every category in the study of the Denver *Post* during the final month of the campaign. There actually was only a very slight and inconclusive advantage in favor of the Republicans.

There are primarily three reasons for this conclusion. First, Eisenhower made his vacation headquarters in Denver, with the natural and understandable result that his presence there called for special coverage. Secondly, this newspaper employed a highly unorthodox system of news play, particularly on its front page. On October 7 and October 8, for example, six stories on Democratic activities, including two banner headlines, appeared on the front page with no mention of the Republicans. Conversely, on October 14 and 15 the Democrats received no front page coverage while three stories, including a banner, were devoted to the Republicans. In the thirty-day study, the Republicans were given four banners, the Democrats three, which provides no evidence of partiality.

Inside page coverage on October 16 and October 24 was comparatively even—14 stories for each party, an eight-to-seven margin for the Republicans in multiple-column headlines, and 180 column-inches for the Republicans, 136 column-inches for the Democrats. But in the November 3 issue the Republicans were given much more space and emphasis, accounting for the wide variation in the final statistics for inside page coverage.

It should be noted that if the special coverage of the Eisenhower train given by a member of the Denver *Post* staff had been balanced with equivalent coverage of Stevenson's activities, this newspaper would have emerged with an excellent record.

CONNECTICUT

HARTFORD TIMES

(Eisenhower)

	Front Page*		Inside Pages**	
	REP.	DEM.	REP.	DEM.
Number of stories	26	34	10	8
Column-inches stories	504½	586	169½	129
Number of photographs	5	6	1	2
Column-inches photographs	116	107	15	19
Multi-column headlines	12	12	5	5
Total column-inches news space	620½	693	184½	148

* No Sunday edition.
** Issue of October 17 substituted for October 16 in study of inside pages because Truman was in Hartford on latter date.

Excellent campaign coverage was evident in the Hartford *Times*, which editorially supported Eisenhower. A front page advantage for the Democrats in news space was balanced by a similar margin in favor of the Republicans in inside pages. Multiple-column headlines on both front and inside pages were equally divided. There was no appreciable difference in the number or size of photographs published.

Both Truman and Eisenhower spoke from the *Times* portico during the period of this survey, and there was no significant difference in the coverage of these two speeches.

No consistent typographical pattern was employed, but there was an attempt at all times to give each party its fair share of space and prominence in display. Most frequently employed were the devices of side-by-side play or shared headlines with two decks dropping from them for evenly played stories. This newspaper demonstrated that it is possible to be fair to both parties without resorting to unimaginative or repetitive makeup.

DELAWARE
WILMINGTON JOURNAL—EVERY EVENING
(Eisenhower)

	Front Page*		Inside Pages	
	REP.	DEM.	REP.	DEM.
Number of stories	36	56	22	17
Column-inches stories	320	406½	175½	137½
Number of photographs	6	7	1	0
Column-inches photographs	82	77	9	0
Multi-column headlines	11	12	0	1
Total column-inches news space	402	483½	184½	137½

* No Sunday edition.

The Wilmington *Journal-Every Evening*, although supporting the candidacy of Eisenhower, gave a greater amount of its front page news space to the Democrats.

There were two factors, however, which tended to equal-ize coverage given to the two parties. First, the inside pages gave approximately the same advantage to the Republicans that the front pages had given to the Democrats. Secondly, the Republicans received better display on the fewer front-page stories in their favor. Of the fourteen top headlines de-voted to the campaign during the period under study, the Republicans had three top headlines exclusively, compared to one for the Democrats, and received first play in eight of the ten shared headlines.

A comparison of treatment accorded the visits of Eisen-hower and Truman four days apart demonstrates this news-paper's fair coverage. Both men received eight-column, two-line banners with two-column decks, a four-column photograph played in identical position, and stories of ap-proximately the same size running down the same columns.

FLORIDA
MIAMI HERALD
(Eisenhower)

	Front Page*		Inside Pages	
	REP.	DEM.	REP.	DEM.
Number of stories	38	54	10	12
Column-inches stories	427½	511	66½	69½
Number of photographs	9	4	4	0
Column-inches photographs	87	41	47	0
Multi-column headlines	14	12	5	4
Total column-inches news space	514½	552	113½	69½

* Issue of October 15 was missing in this study.

The pro-Eisenhower Miami *Herald* followed a policy of giving an advantage to the Democrats in news column space and favoring the Republicans in its photo coverage.

The statistical advantage enjoyed by the Democrats in news treatment can be explained in large part by the fact that Stevenson spoke in Miami during this period while Eisenhower did not. The only other prominent speakers in Miami during the month preceding the election were Kefauver and John Roosevelt, the latter campaigning for the Republican ticket. Treatment of these two campaigners was comparatively equal.

While the Democrats had an advantage in the number of news stories and news space both on the front page and on inside pages, better display and heavier photographic coverage was given to the Republicans. The Miami *Herald* performance was essentially an impartial one.

GEORGIA

ATLANTA JOURNAL

(Stevenson)

	Front Page*		Inside Pages	
	REP.	DEM.	REP.	DEM.
Number of stories	28	33	11	12
Column-inches stories	360	494½	81½	132½
Number of photographs	1	3	2	1
Column-inches photographs	8	31	20	10
Multi-column headlines	12	16	3	6
Total column-inches news space	368	525½	101½	142½

* Includes Sunday *Journal* and *Constitution*.

The Atlanta *Journal*, which announced its support of the candidacy of Governor Stevenson on October 9, gave only slightly better play to the man it editorially supported.

Although photographs were used almost equally for the candidates and their supporters, as the table indicates, the news columns favored the Democrats on both front and inside pages. On the nine occasions in which top play was given to the campaign, Stevenson had three headlines, Eisenhower one; Stevenson got the first of two lines on three occasions, Eisenhower was given the first line two times. The Democrats, therefore, fared slightly better than the Republicans in news display.

It should be noted that the statistical imbalance in this newspaper was largely the result of extensive coverage given to the activities of Truman. The two candidates, Eisenhower and Stevenson, fared approximately the same in the news columns. In many ways this was a very good performance, qualified only by a tendency to give the Democrats slightly better play and coverage in a few issues.

IDAHO
Boise *IDAHO DAILY STATESMAN*
(Eisenhower)

	Front Page		Inside Pages	
	REP.	DEM.	REP.	DEM.
Number of stories	103	103	15	7
Column-inches stories	534½	563	87½	31
Number of photographs	3	0	0	0
Column-inches photographs	32	0	0	0
Multi-column headlines	9	9	0	0
Total column-inches news space	566½	563	87½	31

The Idaho *Daily Statesman*, a supporter of Eisenhower in the 1952 election, was extraordinarily—almost astonishingly—fair in its coverage. Consider these facts:

Same number of front page stories for each party during the one-month period under study and same number of multiple-column headlines for each party.

Column-inches of front page news space separated by only the slimmest of margins, and when photographic coverage is included the two parties are separated by only 3½ column-inches out of a total of 1129½ column-inches.

The small amount of inside page coverage does not hold to this extremely high standard statistically, but this newspaper, as the table shows, reported campaign news predominantly on its front page. This performance stands as an example of newspaper responsibility on the highest level.

The achievement of the Idaho *Daily Statesman*, furthermore, did not rest on dull, unimaginative news treatment. Makeup varied widely from day to day, frequently employing twin or triplet stories off a main headline. The Truman "whistle-stop" campaign was balanced with extensive coverage of the Republican "Truth Squad" which followed him. Readers of this newspaper received an excellent report on the presidential campaign in news columns free of any reflection of editorial partisanship.

ILLINOIS
CHICAGO TRIBUNE
(Eisenhower)

	Front Page		Inside Pages	
	REP.	DEM.	REP.	DEM.
Number of stories	30	15	26	14
Column-inches stories	591	272	381½	216

Number of photographs	0	0	3	1
Column-inches photographs	0	0	37	11
Multi-column headlines	13	7	2	0
Total column-inches news space	591	272	418½	227

News space allotment in favor of the Republicans that ran approximately and consistently two-to-one marked Chicago *Tribune* coverage of the final month of the 1952 campaign.

In addition to the distinct statistical advantage given to the Republicans, there was a considerable difference in display of stories concerning the campaign. The Republicans received thirteen top or secondary eight-column banners, the Democrats were given six.

Further analysis of banner presentation is revealing. Eisenhower, Taft, Nixon, Truman and Stevenson (twice) spoke in Chicago during the period studied, which would indicate that the evenly divided six visits should make a good test case. Here is what happened: Nixon and Eisenhower—top banners; Taft—secondary banner; Stevenson—two secondary banners; Truman—six-column headline.

There were some notable headlines in these issues. One example should suffice. Headline: "Adlai Permits Ex-Convict to Introduce Him." Deck: "Gives Curley the Honor in Boston." (October 27.)

There is no doubt that the thread of the Chicago *Tribune*'s editorial preference ran through its news columns clearly and unmistakably.

INDIANA

INDIANAPOLIS STAR

(Eisenhower)

	Front Page		Inside Pages	
	REP.	DEM.	REP.	DEM.
Number of stories	56	24	28	11
Column-inches stories	707½	209	215½	91
Number of photographs	3	0	4	4
Column-inches photographs	52	0	44	44
Multi-column headlines	45	24	13	6
Total column-inches news space	759½	209	259½	135

The Indianapolis *Star*, as the table clearly shows, gave the Republicans far greater coverage during the final month of the 1952 presidential campaign. Here are additional factors:

In the thirty-day period covered in this study, Republicans were given better front page display on twenty-eight days; only on October 30 and November 2 could the display be considered relatively even.

In the same period, the Republicans were given two eight-column banner headlines, 12 seven-column headlines and one three-column headline; the Democrats received one three-column headline.

Republican activities were well reported on the front page every day; on eight of the 30 days included in this survey there were no stories on Democratic activities.

Although this study was concerned only with news items pertaining to candidates at the national level, it is interesting to note the treatment given by the Indianapolis *Star* to candidates for governor and senator in Indiana. Following are all of the front page headlines pertaining to the state races during the last half of the month of October:

Demos Barring GI Vote: Craig—Schricker Accused Of Neglect; Schricker's Gaming Tax Policy Hit by Jenner (October 16).

Vote GOP To Denounce War, Craig Tells Rally (October 17).

Korea Peace Hopeless Under Democrats: Craig (October 18).

Schricker Says Truman Slurs 'Regrettable' (October 19).

State Demo Leaders Minimize Truman 'Slur' (October 20).

Pro-Ike Worker Fired From Demo Road Job (October 21).

Jenner Hurls Key Questions (October 22).

Jenner Answers Blast Leveled By Stevenson; Craig Blasts Archaic Mental Program Policy; Trustee Jabs At Schricker—Calls 'Pocket Veto' Political Reprisal (October 23).

Jenner Wins Praise From Demo Senator; Demo Victory Means New Wars, Jenner Says (October 24).

Schricker 'Only Chance' To Win, Says McKinney (October 27).

Jenner Raps Stevenson For Korean War Stand (October 28).

Craig Caps Campaign With 16-Point Program; 3 Prominent Hoosier Demos Support Jenner (October 29).

Stalin, Democrats Fear Ike, Jenner Declares (October 31).

The Democratic candidate for governor against Mr. Craig was John A. Watkins.

IOWA

DES MOINES REGISTER

(Eisenhower)

	Front Page		Inside Pages	
	REP.	DEM.	REP.	DEM.
Number of stories	35	30	10	12
Column-inches stories	379½	336	254	335
Number of photographs	3	1	3	2
Column-inches photographs	60	12	54	42
Multi-column headlines	3	5	2	2
Total column-inches news space	439½	348	308	377

Despite the fact that this newspaper gave the candidate it supported more front page space, other factors influencing campaign presentation result in the conclusion that there was no significant partiality in the news columns during the period under study.

The Democrats were given a slight edge in typographical display, receiving five of the eight multi-column headlines devoted exclusively to activities of one party. The survey of inside pages also favored the Democrats in sufficient degree to offset the slight emphasis given to Republican news on the front page, and the fact that Nixon was the only major participant to visit Des Moines in addition to Truman and Taft—who spoke on the same day—also contributed to giving the Republicans a front page statistical advantage in both news and photograph allotment.

The Register frequently grouped campaign news stories under a shared headline with an overline, "The Campaign." When this device was not used, equal play was almost always given to representatives of both parties in the campaign. A large number of speech texts appeared on inside pages.

KENTUCKY

LOUISVILLE COURIER-JOURNAL

(Stevenson)

	Front Page		Inside Pages	
	REP.	DEM.	REP.	DEM.
Number of stories	35	36	17	16
Column-inches stories	449	467½	128½	195
Number of photographs	12	17	0	1
Column-inches photographs	123	167	0	16
Multi-column headlines	10	10	7	11
Total column-inches news space	572	634½	128½	211

Comprehensive and fair reporting of the campaign was apparent in the coverage of the Louisville *Courier-Journal*, which gave editorial support to Stevenson.

The statistical advantage given to coverage of Democratic activities resulted from the visit to Louisville of Wilson Wyatt, Stevenson's campaign manager and the only nationally prominent person to speak in Louisville during this period. Had it not been for this event, the Republicans would have had an equally unimportant front page statistical margin.

A conscious effort to be fair in front page news presentation was evident every day in this newspaper. One typical example is the issue of October 15, in which Eisenhower was given a two-column photograph and two-column headline while Stevenson received a three-column cut with a one-column headline.

Inside page treatment was equally good. A breakdown in

the number of stories on inside pages of the three issues examined shows that on October 16 the Republicans and Democrats each had six stories, on October 24 the Republicans had six and the Democrats five, and on November 3 each party was given five stories. Extensive reporting of Truman's speeches accounted in large part for the space differences on inside pages.

LOUISIANA
NEW ORLEANS TIMES-PICAYUNE
(Independent)

	Front Page		Inside Pages*	
	REP.	DEM.	REP.	DEM.
Number of stories	27	16	20	18
Column-inches stories	284½	183½	206½	245½
Number of photographs	6	4	0	1
Column-inches photographs	69	60	0	16
Multi-column headlines	10	4	4	4
Total column-inches news space	353½	243½	206½	261½

* Issue of October 17 substituted for October 16 in study of inside pages because Eisenhower was still receiving special coverage on his Louisiana visit on latter date.

On Sunday, October 19, 1952, replying editorially on its front page to charges of bias made against it, the *Times-Picayune* said that "it has endeavored to be fair in its news and editorial columns."

This newspaper, in the *Editor & Publisher* poll published November 1, 1952, professed an independent policy in the election campaign. Its claim to fairness in its news columns was substantiated in this study in the categories of photographic treatment and inside page coverage. The *Times-Picayune* would have difficulty, however, proving its point in regard to front page coverage.

Considerably more headline play, stories and news space were devoted to the Republicans than were given to the Democratic side. Sole top play was given to the Republicans on five days and twice to the Democrats. Of three shared top play headlines, Eisenhower was given the first line, Stevenson the second line on each occasion. Eisenhower's visit to New Orleans was treated with appreciably more news column enthusiasm than was Stevenson's appearance only three days earlier, notably including a front page parade route map and schedule of activities only for the Republican candidate.

This front page Republican preponderance, however, was largely offset by inside page coverage which slightly favored the Democrats. This newspaper, which was eminently fair in many aspects of news presentation, did not achieve equal coverage of both parties on its front page.

MAINE
BANGOR DAILY NEWS
(Eisenhower)

	Front Page*		Inside Pages	
	REP.	DEM.	REP.	DEM.
Number of stories	18	18	4	5
Column-inches stories	254	173	21	32½
Number of photographs	0	0	0	0
Column-inches photographs	0	0	0	0
Multi-column headlines	14	13	0	0
Total column-inches news space	254	173	21	32½

* Saturday and Sunday editions of this newspaper are combined.

The Bangor *Daily News* was very fair in the number of front page news stories and multi-column headlines for each party, and although inside pages carried only a few campaign stories they tended to favor the Democrats slightly. The Republicans, however, were given six eight-column headlines—five for Eisenhower and one for McCarthy —while the Democrats received none. There was room for improvement in the allotment of front page news space and banner headline treatment in this newspaper, but there is no conclusive evidence of partiality in the news columns.

MARYLAND

BALTIMORE SUN

(Eisenhower)

	Front Page		Inside Pages	
	REP.	DEM.	REP.	DEM.
Number of stories	63	87	14	20
Column-inches stories	688	936½	196	271
Number of photographs	3	2	3	1
Column-inches photographs	21	7	37	10
Multi-column headlines	45	47	3	7
Total column-inches news space	709	943½	233	281

No favoritism toward the candidate of its choice was found in the Baltimore *Sun*, which supported Eisenhower but gave the Democrats greater coverage during the month before the election.

More stories and a greater amount of news space were devoted to Democratic activities on both front and inside pages, while the Republicans were given slightly better photographic coverage. Multiple-column play was impres-

sively even, particularly on the front page, and the difference in inside page multi-column headline treatment is
modified by the fact that two of the three Eisenhower heads
were banners whereas Stevenson had no inside banners in
the issues examined.

The Democratic statistical advantage was balanced by
slightly better display for the Republican cause. Eisenhower
received four top banner headlines, Stevenson two. Of
eight shared banners (one line to each party), Eisenhower
and Stevenson each received the first line four times. Italic
banners running under the top banner were divided five for
Eisenhower, three for Stevenson, with one shared head
giving the Republicans first mention.

This is a performance above reproach.

MICHIGAN
DETROIT NEWS
(Eisenhower)

	Front Page		Inside Pages	
	REP.	DEM.	REP.	DEM.
Number of stories	30	30	18	10
Column-inches stories	332½	232½	144	132½
Number of photographs	3	1	1	1
Column-inches photographs	36	18	11	16
Multi-column headlines	15	7	5	5
Total column-inches news space	368½	250½	155	148½

Despite the fact that the Republicans were given a
significantly larger amount of front page space, it would be
difficult after any careful appraisal of this newspaper's per-

formance to prove a conscious news column bias during the final month of the 1952 campaign.

Several factors should be taken into consideration. First, both parties were given the same number of front page stories during the period under study. Secondly, inside page coverage showed no significant favoritism toward one party. A third point is that in two front page Eisenhower stories, bold face inserts were employed to call attention to Stevenson stories on inside pages, a device that is not reflected in a statistical compilation but which serves to modify the effect of a front page story. And finally, the fact that Eisenhower made his "I'll go to Korea" announcement in a Detroit speech, with the resulting heavy play, accounts for a large measure of the news and photograph space advantage for the Republicans.

This paper, in a news story reporting the charge of news column bias made against it by a group of American authors, commented in an editor's note that "obviously the 96 authors couldn't have made a study of Detroit *News* coverage and arrived unanimously at a conclusion so at variance with the facts." The editor takes a valid position. If bias existed in this newspaper, it could not be proved by a brief, hurried examination of one week's issues. Even after a careful study of thirty issues, it was not possible in this study to find conclusive evidence of news column bias.

MINNESOTA

MINNEAPOLIS STAR

(Eisenhower)

	Front Page*		Inside Pages	
	REP.	DEM.	REP.	DEM.
Number of stories	29	31	10	15
Column-inches stories	318	327½	192	229½
Number of photographs	1	3	4	2
Column-inches photographs	18	45	25	11
Multi-column headlines	3	2	4	5
Total column-inches news space	336	372½	217	240½

* No Sunday edition.

This newspaper demonstrated a high degree of impartiality in its campaign coverage.

Eisenhower, whose candidacy was endorsed editorially, had slightly less front page news and photo space than his opponent during the one-month period under study, but his cause had a slight advantage in multi-column headlines. In the three editions examined for inside page coverage, Eisenhower had a small photographic advantage but was given fewer news stories, less news space, and fewer multi-column headlines. Most important, perhaps, is the fact that the statistical differences in all categories are insignificant, evidence that there was a determined effort on the part of this newspaper to be scrupulously fair in its coverage.

Since the top display position was rarely used for campaign news, an analysis of headline construction is interesting. Of seven shared two-line headlines, Eisenhower was given the first line five times, Stevenson twice. Of shared

three-line heads, Stevenson had the first 1½ lines four
times, Eisenhower three times; still another three-line head
was divided with the first line to Eisenhower, the second
and third lines to Stevenson. This varied news display also
shows that it is possible to use a dynamic typographical
display and still be fair to both sides in a political campaign.

MISSISSIPPI

JACKSON CLARION-LEDGER

(Stevenson)

	Front Page		Inside Pages	
	REP.	DEM.	REP.	DEM.
Number of stories	38	40	4	5
Column-inches stories	392	423½	17½	35½
Number of photographs	1	1	0	0
Column-inches photographs	3	3	0	0
Multi-column headlines	9	11	0	1.
Total column-inches news space	395	426½	17½	35½

The *Clarion-Ledger*, which gave mild support to the
Stevenson-Sparkman ticket editorially, showed impartiality
in its news columns. The statistical advantage enjoyed by
the Democrats in news coverage was so slight as to be imperceptible to readers, and this performance is even more
impressive when one considers the multiple cross-currents
of Mississippi politics.

Inside pages carried only a small amount of campaign
news, and the statistical margin of the Democrats hinged
on a single long story about Democratic demands that
Nixon reveal his income tax returns.

The only eight-column banner devoted to campaign

news during this period was one reporting "Sen. Byrd Flouts Stevenson," a story hardly calculated to aid the cause espoused editorially by the *Clarion-Ledger*. In its selection of top play stories, this newspaper emerged with a perfect record: One three-line headline divided between Democrats and Republicans; one headline reporting Gov. White's pro-Stevenson sentiments balancing the aforementioned Byrd headline; and one headline each to Stevenson and Eisenhower.

MISSOURI

ST. LOUIS POST-DISPATCH
(Stevenson)

	Front Page		Inside Pages	
	REP.	DEM.	REP.	DEM.
Number of stories	68	80	38	42
Column-inches stories	809	1010	380	661½
Number of photographs	9	11	9	10
Column-inches photographs	99	127	106	131
Multi-column headlines	11	14	3	10
Total column-inches news space	908	1137	486	792½

A slight but inconclusive news emphasis in favor of the candidate it editorially supported was evident in the coverage of the final month of the 1952 campaign by the pro-Stevenson St. Louis *Post-Dispatch*.

The figures in the table, however, do not tell the full story. For instance, Stevenson and Truman were the only major principals to speak in St. Louis during the period under study, and reporting of these local events greatly increased the statistical differences between the two parties in front page coverage. Similarly, the three issues chosen for inside page examination included five Stevenson texts and one Truman text, compared to two Eisenhower texts; this proved to be of no significance after a survey of additional issues demonstrated that the number of Republican speech texts frequently outnumbered Democratic texts. Tabulation of inside page statistics excluding texts showed the Republicans with 35 stories totaling 273 inches, the Democrats with 36 stories totaling 392 inches. Photographic coverage was virtually equal, but the fact remains that the amount of space for each party on inside pages of this newspaper tended to favor the Democrats.

Campaign news received top play in 27 of the 30 issues in this study, and headline treatment also favored the Democratic cause. The Democrats received higher position in 16 shared headlines, the Republicans in nine. The Democrats were given the entire top headline on two occasions, the Republicans received no top headline play exclusively.

Further analysis of the tremendous volume of campaign news carried in this newspaper indicates that it was during the first 12 days and last seven days of this 30-day period that the *Post-Dispatch* gave more coverage to the Democrats. During the period of October 18 through October 28, the front page performance was exceptional: Both parties had twenty-eight stories, both had first play in shared banner headlines five times, both had two exclusive multi-column headlines; the Republicans had 33 column-inches of photographic space compared to 61 for the Democrats, and the Republicans received 352 column-inches of news space to 349½ column-inches for the Democrats.

An example of poor front page coverage, however, was the November 2 issue which had a three-line, five-column headline:

TRUMAN HERE: 'WE'RE GOING TO WIN'

STEVENSON HITS 'SQUALID TACTICS'

M'CARTHY 'FALSEHOODS' ANSWERED

Dropping off these lines were three single-column decks on speeches by Mitchell, Stevenson and Truman, and a two-column photograph of Truman in St. Louis. Under the Truman cut was another two-column story. Eisenhower, with the election two days away, was given only a single-column headline and story in the third column. It was this kind of occasional performance which marred an otherwise unusually extensive and fair report of the campaign.

MONTANA

GREAT FALLS TRIBUNE

(Stevenson)

	Front Page		Inside Pages	
	REP.	DEM.	REP.	DEM.
Number of stories	33	70	13	14
Column-inches stories	244	632½	75½	148½
Number of photographs	2	9	0	1
Column-inches photographs	20	118	0	4
Multi-column headlines	16	36	3	7
Total column-inches news space	264	750½	75½	152½

The news columns of the pro-Stevenson Great Falls *Tribune* gave a decided advantage to the Democrats in the last month of the presidential campaign. Republican

speeches and activities were inundated by a flood of stories
and photographs emphasizing the Democratic cause, and
the Eisenhower campaign was given little more than token
coverage.

Aside from the Eisenhower trip into Montana, which
was given adequate prominence, the Republican presidential candidate was consistently overlooked in presentation of campaign news. His speeches were given front page
coverage only on October 6 and 7—while he was in Montana—October 14, October 20, October 30, November 1,
November 2 and November 3. Stevenson, on the other
hand, was extensively reported on the front page on twenty-
two of the thirty days covered in this study.

The only Republican pictures to appear on the front
page were two Nixon photos which appeared during the
vice-presidential candidate's visit to Great Falls. There were
no photographs of Eisenhower. Stevenson was featured in
seven front page photographs, Truman in two.

This newspaper was mild in its editorial support of the
Democratic ticket. The news columns, however, did not
hide the editorial preference.

NEBRASKA
OMAHA WORLD-HERALD
(Eisenhower)

	Front Page		Inside Pages	
	REP.	DEM.	REP.	DEM.
Number of stories	40	33	7	4
Column-inches stories	440	328	34	26½
Number of photographs	0	0	0	0

Column-inches photographs	0	0	0	0
Multi-column headlines	5	0	1	0
Total column-inches news space	440	328	34	26½

A slight but inconclusive news emphasis in favor of the Republican party was found in the one-month study of this newspaper.

The handling of front page news showed a space and display advantage for the Republicans, who were given top position the five times in which the top story of the day was devoted exclusively to the activities of one party. There was no photographic coverage in the issues examined, and inside page treatment of the campaign was almost negligible (the one multi-column head and slight advantage for the Republicans resulted from a speech in Nebraska by a Republican senator).

Although there is no conclusive evidence of partiality in news columns, this newspaper's performance clearly was not above reproach. It was unfortunate that the *World-Herald* did not more frequently employ the shared headline with decks and stories dropping from it, a device it used with effectiveness and fairness on several occasions.

NEW YORK

NEW YORK TIMES

(Eisenhower)

	Front Page		Inside Pages	
	REP.	DEM.	REP.	DEM.
Number of stories	46	70	43	36
Column-inches stories	532	799	477½	592
Number of photographs	11	11	4	5

Column-inches photographs	180	180	52	76
Multi-column headlines	16	17	4	6
Total column-inches news space	712	979	529½	668

Extensive coverage of Truman, particularly during his two visits to New York City, accounted for the statistical advantage for the Democrats in this newspaper.

Display, photographic treatment and inside page coverage, however, were extremely fair to both parties.

Of the 10 multi-column headlines in the top position, the Democrats had two exclusively, the Republicans none; the Democrats and Republicans each had the first two lines of three-line heads on three occasions, and the Republicans had the first line of two-line heads on the two days in which this presentation was employed. The top of the eighth column, normally considered the best position when multi-column top play is not used, went to the Democrats eight times, to the Republicans seven times.

Truman and Eisenhower were in New York twice during the period under study, Stevenson and Nixon once. There was no discernible difference in treatment of these events. Photographic coverage, as the table shows, was remarkably fair. The seeming advantage enjoyed by the Democrats in inside pages disappears when space allotted to texts of speeches is eliminated from consideration. Statistics on inside page coverage, excluding texts, shows forty stories with 300 column-inches for the Republicans, thirty stories with 292½ column-inches for the Democrats. When photographic statistics are included, there is a difference of only 14½ column-inches in favor of the Democrats—368½ to 352—which is indeed an extraordinary performance.

NORTH DAKOTA
FARGO FORUM
(Eisenhower)

	Front Page		Inside Pages	
	REP.	DEM.	REP.	DEM.
Number of stories	57	63	8	11
Column-inches stories	470	546½	62	112
Number of photographs	5	2	1	1
Column-inches photographs	57	21	18	18
Multi-column headlines	17	13	0	3
Total column-inches news space	527	567½	80	130

Consciously fair coverage marked the performance of this newspaper during the presidential campaign. The Democrats were given a slightly larger number of front page and inside stories and enjoyed more news column space. The Republicans, on the other hand, were given slightly more photographic coverage and better display. It would be almost impossible to detect from the news pages of this paper that its editorial preference was for the Republicans.

It is significant that the Fargo *Forum* conscientiously stood guard on its own conduct during the heated campaign, as demonstrated by a front page editorial on October 7. Pointing out that extensive coverage was given to the Fargo visits of Truman and Eisenhower, it added that "in retrospect, it should interest both our Republican and Democratic readers to compare the coverage of each story."

Then, employing in part the quantitative methods used in this study, the newspaper editorially reported:

The Truman stories occupied 218 column inches of type, pictures 149 column inches, or a total of 367 inches. Ike's stories ran to 223 inches of type and 164 inches of pictures, a total of 387 column inches.

So, of more than two pages devoted each to the Truman and Eisenhower visits, the General had only one more column of space than the President.

These North Dakota speeches by Truman and Eisenhower took place before the period included in this study and do not, of course, affect the statistical compilation included in this survey. But on the basis of its subsequent handling of campaign news, it is evident that this newspaper can take pride in its news presentation throughout the entire political campaign.

It should be pointed out that in addition to the small multi-column headline advantage given to the Republicans, the only two banner headlines in the thirty-day period were devoted to the Eisenhower cause. But it was offset by the greater amount of news space for the Democrats on both the front and inside pages.

OREGON

PORTLAND OREGONIAN

(Eisenhower)

	Front Page		Inside Pages	
	REP.	DEM.	REP.	DEM.
Number of stories	42	43	12	11
Column-inches stories	531	520½	134	139
Number of photographs	7	8	2	2
Column-inches photographs	118	77	25	18
Multi-column headlines	19	16	4	6
Total column-inches news space	649	597½	159	157

The Portland *Oregonian* was remarkably impartial in its coverage of the 1952 presidential campaign, demonstrating an even-handed presentation of the news throughout the entire one-month period studied.

Making the statistics even more impressive were two factors: 1) Eisenhower was in Portland during this period, Stevenson was not; 2) headline and display performance was equally good.

Sparkman was the only other major principal in the campaign to speak in Portland during the month preceding the election, and he received extensive coverage.

If the local visits of these two candidates were omitted from the study, the Democrats actually would enjoy a decided statistical advantage in every category of front page presentation. The study of inside page coverage, uninfluenced by these visits, revealed extremely fair coverage.

Excluding play resulting from Eisenhower's appearance in Portland, Democrats and Republicans received sole top position once each. Other large headlines, when shared by persons of both parties or appearing in lesser display position, showed no tendency to favor one party over the other by typographical emphasis.

No reader of the *Oregonian*, regardless of his political preference, could justifiably have been offended by the reporting of the campaign in the news columns of this paper.

PENNSYLVANIA
PHILADELPHIA EVENING BULLETIN
(Eisenhower)

	Front Page		Inside Pages	
	REP.	DEM.	REP.	DEM.
Number of stories	55	65	21	23
Column-inches stories	438½	488½	275	363
Number of photographs	5	5	3	3
Column-inches photographs	102	112	54	61
Multi-column headlines	8	10	7	9
Total column-inches news space	540½	600½	329	424

Readers of this newspaper which editorially supported Eisenhower were given a comprehensive and very fair report of the campaign in the news columns. The Democrats were given slightly more news and photographic space and more multi-column headlines than were the Republicans on both the front and inside pages, but the difference would be imperceptible to most readers.

In addition to the well-balanced news coverage which was uninfluenced by editorial page policies, the *Bulletin* ran a large number of special articles and texts of speeches by major principals in the campaign. Particularly noteworthy is the fact that the study of inside pages included the issue of October 24, which reported the visit of Sen. Taft to Philadelphia. In spite of this, the Democrats enjoyed an advantage of coverage in the news columns of inside pages.

Eisenhower, Stevenson and Truman made major speeches in Philadelphia. Reporting of the three events was similar in display and space allotments, with no significant difference in the statistical breakdown.

An analysis of headline treatment on top-play stories offers additional evidence of fairness on the part of this newspaper. The Republicans were given sole top position on two occasions, the Democrats once. The first two lines of three-line heads went to the Democrats twice, to the Republicans once. The first half of two- or three-line heads went to the Democrats five times, to the Republicans four times. This performance is no accident; it can be said with assurance that the *Bulletin* made certain that both sides had a fair hearing in its news columns.

SOUTH DAKOTA
SIOUX FALLS ARGUS-LEADER
(Eisenhower)

	Front Page		Inside Pages	
	REP.	DEM.	REP.	DEM.
Number of stories	53	43	11	5
Column-inches stories	533½	376½	78½	21½
Number of photographs	4	3	1	0
Column-inches photographs	50	33	12	0
Multi-column headlines	13	8	0	0
Total column-inches news space	583½	409½	90½	21½

Both in its allotment of space and display of news this newspaper showed partiality toward the Republican party, which it editorially endorsed.

The Republicans not only received more news and photographic space on the front and inside pages, but they also were awarded prominent display almost exclusively. The statistics on allotment of multi-column headlines tell only part of the story; not shown by the figures is the fact that Eisenhower was given seven banner headlines and one

six-column headline during the period under study while
the Democrats had nothing larger than one three-column
headline (and that a deck under an Eisenhower banner).
Not included, incidentally, was one Eisenhower eight-
column banner which reported on a professional poll, a
story classification not included in this study.

TENNESSEE
MEMPHIS COMMERCIAL APPEAL
(Eisenhower)

	Front Page		Inside Pages*	
	REP.	DEM.	REP.	DEM.
Number of stories	52	60	10	9
Column-inches stories	588	601½	116½	104½
Number of photographs	4	1	1	3
Column-inches photographs	85	13	14	47
Multi-column headlines	8	8	1	1
Total column-inches news space	673	614½	130½	151½

* Issue of October 17 substituted for October 16 in study of inside
pages because Eisenhower was in Memphis on latter date.

Campaign coverage in this newspaper which editorially
supported Eisenhower was very fair and tended, if any-
thing, to give the Democrats better coverage than the
Republicans.

Eisenhower was the only one of the five major principals
to visit Memphis during the period under study, and if the
special coverage properly given to that event were subtracted from Republican totals, the Democrats would enjoy
an even greater advantage. The Stevenson campaign was
given the larger portion of front page news space and was
given equal photographic coverage if the three Eisenhower

pictures related to his Memphis visit are disregarded. Multi-column treatment was equal. Top play was given solely to Eisenhower five times—three of them at the time of his trip to Memphis—and to Stevenson twice. In the frequently used three-line top play, the Republicans were given the first two lines 13 times, the Democrats on seven occasions. This slight display advantage for the Republicans in part offsets heavier news space play for the Democrats.

Therefore, aside from the Eisenhower appearance in Memphis, the *Commercial Appeal's* front page had many more Democratic stories, much more news space devoted to the Democrats, equal photographic coverage, equal multi-column display, a slightly better top display for the Republicans. Its inside pages hardly could have been more fair. There was no evidence in the *Commercial Appeal* news columns of its editorial preference for the candidacy of Eisenhower.

TEXAS

DALLAS MORNING NEWS

(Eisenhower)

| | Front Page | | Inside Pages* | |
	REP.	DEM.	REP.	DEM.
Number of stories	55	56	16	12
Column-inches stories	540	499½	137½	117
Number of photographs	3	3	1	0
Column-inches photographs	83	58	10	0
Multi-column headlines	16	12	5	2
Total column-inches news space	623	557½	147½	117

* Issue of October 23 substituted for October 16 in study of inside pages because Eisenhower was in Dallas on latter date.

The Republican party was given more space in the news
columns of this paper during the month preceding the 1952
election, but the advantage it enjoyed was a slight one.
More important than the fact that the Eisenhower campaign received more news and photographic space and
more multi-column headlines was the decided emphasis on
reporting the G.O.P. activities. Of the 11 stories in the top
position devoted exclusively to one party, the Republicans
were given eight, the Democrats three. Positions of stories
on the front page also generally favored the Republicans.
Nevertheless, the Stevenson visit to Dallas was given
slightly better front page play than the Eisenhower appearance two days earlier. Eisenhower was reported with a
three-column headline, a three-column photograph (12½
inches deep) and another story for a total of 72½ inches;
Stevenson received a four-column headline, a four-column
photograph (7½ inches deep) and three other stories for a
total of 79½ inches. There is no evidence of favoritism in
this comparison, which in part offsets the typographical
emphasis on the front page and allotment of news and
photographic space on both front and inside pages.

UTAH

Salt Lake City DESERET NEWS

(Independent)

	Front Page*		Inside Pages	
	REP.	DEM.	REP.	DEM.
Number of stories	29	36	4	3
Column-inches stories	297	335	44	25½
Number of photographs	6	5	2	2
Column-inches photographs	101	90	6	6

| Multi-column headlines | 6 | 7 | 1 | 0 |
| Total column-inches news space | 398 | 425 | 50 | 31½ |

* No Sunday edition.

"The *Deseret News*," wrote President McKay of the Church of Jesus Christ of Latter-day Saints in an announcement in this newspaper on October 6, "is the organ of the church, it will be equally fair and impartial in the treatment of both political parties."

The *Deseret News* lived up to that responsibility. The slight Democratic advantage in front page news treatment was offset by a slight Republican pictorial advantage and by an equally slight margin for the Republicans in inside page news treatment.

Both presidential candidates spoke in Salt Lake City during the period under study and treatment of them was virtually identical in the *Deseret News* columns. Truman and Taft also were given similar coverage during their visits to Salt Lake City.

This newspaper used both balanced play under a general headline and separate story display. In the latter case the stories almost always appeared with similar one-column headlines in roughly equivalent positions.

VERMONT

BURLINGTON FREE PRESS

(Eisenhower)

	Front Page*		Inside Pages	
	REP.	DEM.	REP.	DEM.
Number of stories	34	55	0	0
Column-inches stories	437	614½	0	0

Number of photographs	13	6	0	0
Column-inches photographs	168	54	0	0
Multi-column headlines	13	16	0	0
Total column-inches news space	605	668½	0	0

* No Sunday edition.

Impartial reporting of campaign news marked the performance of this newspaper. As the table shows, the Democrats were given more news stories and news column space, and received slightly more multi-column headlines. The Republicans, on the other hand, had more than twice as many photographs filling more than three times as many column-inches of space. Position of major stories favored neither party. There were no campaign news stories on inside pages.

Although this is an unusual method of news presentation, there is clearly no evidence of partiality on the part of this newspaper. It editorially supported Eisenhower, but Stevenson was given more news column space.

VIRGINIA
RICHMOND TIMES-DISPATCH
(Eisenhower)

| | Front Page | | Inside Pages | |
	REP.	DEM.	REP.	DEM.
Number of stories	46	66	23	20
Column-inches stories	504	674½	221	224
Number of photographs	10	8	2	1
Column-inches photographs	76	60	17	5
Multi-column headlines	9	12	9	6
Total column-inches news space	580	734½	238	229

Despite its editorial support of Eisenhower, the Richmond *Times-Dispatch* devoted more news space on its front page to the Democratic cause than it did to the Republicans, largely because of extensive coverage devoted to Truman. There was a slight but insignificant advantage for the Republicans in photographic coverage. News play was comprehensive and excellently handled. Headline play favored the Republicans, balancing the greater amount of news space devoted to the Democrats. The most common type of top play was a three-line head, and the Republicans were given the first two lines on four occasions, the Democrats twice. The Republicans were given all three lines three times, the Democrats once. Of six shared top-play headlines, the Republicans were given first mention five times, the Democrats once. Inside pages were very fair.

There is no evidence of partiality in this generally excellent performance, although coverage would have been improved if this newspaper had given more news space and less display emphasis to the Republicans.

WASHINGTON

SEATTLE POST-INTELLIGENCER

(Eisenhower)

	Front Page		Inside Pages	
	REP.	DEM.	REP.	DEM.
Number of stories	27	23	13	16
Column-inches stories	307	227	98	123½
Number of photographs	4	3	0	0
Column-inches photographs	86	41	0	0
Multi-column headlines	9	4	6	5
Total column-inches news space	393	268	98	123½

Eisenhower was the only principal to speak in Seattle during the period under study, and therefore the space advantage for the Republicans in this newspaper required adjustment. Elimination of the October 6 and October 7 editions, which reported on the visit, would result in even distribution of news and photographic display for the two parties. The Republican presidential candidate was given three stories totaling 57½ inches, one six-column photograph taking 45 column-inches of space, and two multi-column headlines. If these figures are subtracted from the Republican total (the Democrats received no front page space during these two days) the news and photographic statistics would be virtually equal for the remaining twenty-eight days.

Despite the fact that after October 8 comparatively equal space was devoted to the two parties, this newspaper gave an advantage to the Republicans in its display. Of five stories receiving top play and reporting exclusively on one candidate, four were devoted to Eisenhower and one to Stevenson. Eisenhower also was given the only two second play stories (top left) which were devoted solely to one candidate, and Republican activities generally received better headline and position display throughout the period. Inside page coverage showed no significant bias, the Democrats having a slight advantage in number of stories and news space.

WEST VIRGINIA
CHARLESTON GAZETTE
(Stevenson)

	Front Page		Inside Pages	
	REP.	DEM.	REP.	DEM.
Number of stories	42	71	10	9
Column-inches stories	258	472	72½	74½
Number of photographs	9	11	0	1
Column-inches photographs	74	101	0	11
Multi-column headlines	4	15	3	3
Total column-inches news space	332	573	72½	85½

Far greater coverage of the candidate this newspaper editorially supported marked its front page reporting of the campaign.

The Democrats were given the benefit of many more stories, much more space, better photographic coverage, and almost four times as many multi-column headlines. Even taking into account the appearance of Sparkman in Charleston during this period would not appreciably diminish the statistical advantage given to the Stevenson campaign. Inside page coverage, however, was fair.

Special note should be taken of photographic coverage on the front page. The same photo of Dewey, showing him with a grin that could not be called flattering, was used three times within a 12-day period. The cutline on the photograph on one occasion referred to Dewey as Eisenhower's "political mentor." Readers who protested in the letters column against this type of front page reporting probably noted with interest that although the photograph in question was not used again, Dewey appeared with

Eisenhower in two of the four photographs of Republican activities which later appeared.

WISCONSIN

MILWAUKEE JOURNAL

(Stevenson)

	Front Page		Inside Pages	
	REP.	DEM.	REP.	DEM.
Number of stories	14	21	11	14
Column-inches stories	195	329	139	204½
Number of photographs	0	1	3	2
Column-inches photographs	0	30	23	30
Multi-column headlines	3	6	1	3
Total column-inches news space	195	359	162	234½

The Democratic cause received only slightly better coverage in this pro-Stevenson newspaper.

The statistical and display advantage enjoyed by Stevenson is evident in the table. The Democrats also were given slightly better top play, three headlines to one. In shared top play headlines, Eisenhower received the first of two lines on the two days in which this style was employed. Stevenson had two second-play headlines to Eisenhower's one.

· The statistics and analysis should be tempered by the fact that Stevenson was the only principal to speak in Milwaukee during the period under study. As a result of his visits to Madison and Milwaukee, he received six stories with three multi-column headlines for a total of 94½ inches, and a five-column photograph taking 30 column-inches of space. When these figures are taken into consideration in the statistical analysis, this newspaper showed no front page favoritism for the candidate of its choice. However, the statistics on inside page coverage, uninfluenced in this study by the Stevenson visit, show a slight favoritism for the Democrats.